July 2013

DRUG COMPOUNDING

Clear Authority and More Reliable Data Needed to Strengthen FDA Oversight

GAO Highlights

Highlights of GAO-13-702, a report to congressional requesters

DRUG COMPOUNDING

Clear Authority and More Reliable Data Needed to Strengthen FDA Oversight

Why GAO Did This Study

Drug compounding is the process by which a pharmacist combines, mixes, or alters ingredients to create a drug tailored to the medical needs of an individual. An outbreak of fungal meningitis in 2012 linked to contaminated compounded drugs has raised concerns about state and federal oversight of drug compounding. GAO was asked to update its 2003 testimony on drug compounding. Specifically, this report addresses (1) the status of FDA's authority to oversee drug compounding, and the gaps, if any, between state and federal authority; (2) how FDA has used its data and authority to oversee drug compounding; and (3) the actions taken or planned by states or national pharmacy organizations to improve oversight of drug compounding. GAO reviewed relevant statutes and guidance; reviewed FDA data; and interviewed officials from FDA, national pharmacy organizations, and four states with varied geography, population, and pharmacy regulations.

What GAO Recommends

To help ensure that the entities that compound drugs have appropriate oversight, Congress should consider clarifying FDA's authority to oversee drug compounding. In addition, FDA should ensure its databases collect reliable and timely data on inspections associated with compounded drugs, and differentiate drug compounders from manufacturers. HHS's comments support the need to clarify FDA's authority, and stated that the information in its inspection database could be improved and that it would consider whether it can differentiate compounding pharmacies from manufacturers.

View GAO-13-702. For more information, contact Marcia Crosse at (202) 512-7114 or crossem@gao.gov.

What GAO Found

The authority of the Food and Drug Administration (FDA), an agency within the Department of Health and Human Services (HHS), to oversee drug compounding is unclear. Two federal circuit court decisions have resulted in differing FDA authority in different parts of the country. According to FDA officials, these inconsistent decisions and the agency's limited inspection authority over pharmacies have created challenges in FDA's ability to inspect and take enforcement action against entities engaging in drug compounding. For example, from 2002 through 2012, in order to inspect some facilities engaged in drug compounding, FDA officials said they had to obtain 11 warrants to gain access to drug compounders' facilities that had challenged FDA's inspection authority. GAO also found that while FDA and national pharmacy organization officials generally agreed that states regulate the practice of pharmacy and FDA regulates drug manufacturing, there was no consensus on whether compounding drugs in large quantities—in anticipation of individual prescriptions or without prescriptions—and selling those drugs across state lines falls within the practice of pharmacy or is a type of drug manufacturing that should be overseen by FDA. This lack of consensus and differing FDA authority to oversee compounded drugs across the country has resulted in gaps in oversight of drug compounding.

FDA lacks timely and reliable information to oversee the entities that compound drugs, but has found problems through its limited oversight. Specifically, FDA's inspection database cannot identify all of the agency's inspections of compounding pharmacies, or the final classification of inspection results, for all of the inspections. Until 2013, FDA limited its inspections of compounding pharmacies to those conducted in response to complaints or adverse events. However, the agency recently inspected compounding pharmacies that it identified as posing a significant threat to public health from poor sterile drug production practices in the past and found problems, such as concerns about a lack of sterility, which resulted in recalls of compounded drugs. In addition, drug manufacturers are required to register with FDA and are subject to FDA's inspection and drug approval processes; pharmacies meeting certain requirements are generally exempt from registration. However, some compounding pharmacies may have registered with FDA to market themselves as "FDA-registered" which may lead some purchasers to assume that FDA has inspected or approved their compounded drugs; whereas, according to FDA officials, this is generally not the case.

The states GAO reviewed—California, Connecticut, Florida, and Iowa—have each taken actions to enhance their oversight of drug compounding. For example, Florida required all pharmacies—both those located in the state and out-of-state that sell drugs in Florida—to notify the board of their compounding activities. In addition, national pharmacy organizations have undertaken efforts to help states oversee drug compounding. For example, a national pharmacy organization is working with Iowa to inspect out-of-state pharmacies that ship drugs into the state. However, according to national pharmacy organizations and officials from state boards of pharmacy, some states do not have the resources to inspect pharmacies on a regular basis. Instead, these states inspect pharmacies only in response to a complaint or a reported adverse drug event.

Contents

Figure

Abbreviations

FACTS	Field Accomplishments and Compliance Tracking System
FDA	Food and Drug Administration
FDAMA	Food and Drug Administration Modernization Act of 1997
FDCA	Federal Food, Drug, and Cosmetic Act
HHS	Department of Health and Human Services
NABP	National Association of Boards of Pharmacy
OIG	Office of Inspector General
PCAB	Pharmacy Compounding Accreditation Board
USP	The United States Pharmacopeial Convention

GAO
U.S. GOVERNMENT ACCOUNTABILITY OFFICE

441 G St. N.W.
Washington, DC 20548

July 31, 2013

The Honorable Elijah Cummings
Ranking Member
Committee on Oversight and Government Reform
House of Representatives

The Honorable John Tierney
Ranking Member
Subcommittee on National Security
Committee on Oversight and Government Reform
House of Representatives

Drug compounding is the process by which a pharmacist or doctor combines, mixes, or alters ingredients to create a drug tailored to the medical needs of an individual patient. Compounding, a traditional component of the practice of pharmacy, is typically used to prepare drugs that are not commercially available, such as a drug for a patient who is allergic to an ingredient in a mass-produced pharmaceutical product.[1] Traditionally, state pharmacy regulatory bodies (e.g., boards of pharmacy) regulate pharmacy practice, including drug compounding activities, through state laws and regulations. The Food and Drug Administration (FDA) is the agency within the Department of Health and Human Services (HHS) responsible for assuring the safety and effectiveness of drugs marketed in the United States.[2] Under the Federal Food, Drug, and Cosmetic Act (FDCA), and its implementing regulations, FDA approves new drugs and regulates the manufacture, marketing, and distribution of pharmaceutical products.[3]

An outbreak of fungal meningitis in 2012 linked to contaminated compounded drugs—resulting in over 60 deaths and hundreds of people becoming ill—has led to questions about the safety and quality of

---

[1] While drug compounding is often referred to as "pharmacy compounding," physicians may compound drugs in certain instances. The focus of this review is drug compounding by pharmacies.

[2] FDA is responsible for assuring the safety and effectiveness of these drugs regardless of whether they are manufactured in the United States or abroad.

[3] 21 U.S.C. §§ 301 *et seq.*

GAO-13-702 Drug Compounding

compounded drugs, and raised concerns about state and federal oversight of drug compounding.[4] Concerns have also been raised by FDA and others, including members of Congress and public health advocates, that some pharmacies are going beyond traditional drug compounding by producing large quantities of compounded drugs without prescriptions for individual patients, and selling those compounded drugs to facilities in multiple states. Many believe that these types of pharmacies are manufacturing drugs under the guise of compounding without meeting safety and other requirements with which drug manufacturers must comply.

You asked us to update our 2003 testimony on drug compounding.[5] Specifically, this report addresses (1) the status of FDA's authority to oversee drug compounding, and the gaps, if any, between state and federal authority to oversee drug compounding; (2) how FDA has used its data and authority to oversee drug compounding; and (3) the actions taken or planned by states or national pharmacy organizations to improve oversight of drug compounding.

To describe the status of FDA's authority to oversee drug compounding and any gaps between state and federal authority, we reviewed FDCA provisions pertaining to drug compounding and other relevant federal statutes, regulations, and guidance documents on federal oversight of drug compounding, including FDA's 2002 compliance policy guide on drug compounding. We also reviewed other relevant FDA documents, and interviewed FDA officials on any gaps or proposed actions to address gaps, or to clarify federal and state authority. We selected four states— California, Connecticut, Florida, and Iowa—and reviewed documents, and interviewed officials from state regulatory bodies in each of these states.[6] (App. I contains information on the four states.) In addition, we reviewed documents, and interviewed officials from national organizations

---

[4]The contaminated product was traced to a compounding pharmacy in Massachusetts, which had shipped approximately 17,000 vials of a contaminated injectable steroid to 23 states. According to the Centers for Disease Control and Prevention, as of July 1, 2013, 749 individuals who received the contaminated steroid injections became ill with fungal meningitis or other types of infections, and 61 of them have died.

[5]See GAO, *Prescription Drugs: State and Federal Oversight of Drug Compounding by Pharmacies,* GAO-04-195T (Washington, D.C.: Oct. 23, 2003).

[6]We selected four states based on variations in geography, population, organization of pharmacy regulatory bodies, and pharmacy compounding laws and regulations.

representing pharmacies and pharmacists—including the American Pharmacists Association, American Society of Health-System Pharmacists, International Academy of Compounding Pharmacists, and National Community Pharmacists Association—and other organizations, including the National Association of Boards of Pharmacy (NABP) and the United States Pharmacopeial Convention (USP).[7] We also reviewed reports and studies related to oversight of drug compounding, and interviewed officials involved in those studies, including those from the Congressional Research Service and the HHS Office of Inspector General (OIG).

To examine how FDA has used its data and authority to oversee drug compounding, we reviewed documents and interviewed FDA officials—including officials in the Center for Drug Evaluation and Research, Office of Regulatory Affairs, and Office of the Chief Counsel—regarding data FDA collects on compounded drugs, the entities that compound them, and FDA inspections of those entities. Specifically, we examined data related to drug compounding from (1) FDA's Drug Registration and Listing System on entities that compound drugs that registered with FDA in its drug manufacturer database, and (2) FDA's Field Accomplishments and Compliance Tracking System (FACTS) on inspections of entities that compound drugs. We also interviewed FDA officials on the availability and limitations of FDA's data on adverse events associated with compounded drugs. We compared FDA's data on compounded drugs and the entities that compound them, including FDA's inspections and outcomes of those inspections, to standards described in *Standards for Internal Control in the Federal Government*—which specifies that relevant, reliable, and timely information be available for management decision making and external reporting purposes.[8] We also reviewed

---

[7]NABP is a professional association that assists its member state boards of pharmacy and jurisdictions in developing, implementing, and enforcing uniform standards for the purpose of protecting the public health. USP is a scientific nonprofit organization that sets standards for the identity, strength, quality, and purity of medicines, food ingredients, and dietary supplements. For this report, we refer to these organizations, including those representing pharmacies and pharmacists, as national pharmacy organizations.

[8]These standards provide an overall framework for establishing and maintaining internal controls; and for identifying and addressing major performance and management challenges, and areas at greatest risk of fraud, waste, abuse, and mismanagement. See GAO, *Standards for Internal Control in the Federal Government*, GAO/AIMD-00-21.3.1 (Washington, D.C.: November 1999), and its supplemental guide, *Internal Control Management and Evaluation Tool*, GAO-01-1008G (Washington, D.C.: August 2001).

information on FDA's efforts in 2013 to conduct inspections of entities that, according to the agency, were known to have produced sterile compounded drugs in the past. To assess the reliability of the FDA data, we reviewed FDA guidance and related documentation; interviewed knowledgeable agency officials; and viewed data FDA made available from these databases on its website. We determined that the data were sufficiently reliable for purposes of our report.

To identify actions planned or taken by states or national pharmacy organizations, we reviewed state laws and regulations, and proposed changes to state laws and regulations, in the four states we selected. For each state, we reviewed documents and interviewed representatives of the states' pharmacy regulatory bodies regarding actions taken or planned relating to the oversight of drug compounding, the implications of existing and proposed state laws and regulations, and the challenges state regulatory bodies face in overseeing drug compounding. We also discussed the states' pharmacy inspection and enforcement activities, as well as state efforts to collect pharmacy data. In addition, we reviewed surveys of states—for example, results of surveys of states to determine the number requiring compliance with USP provisions for sterile compounding. We also reviewed documents and interviewed officials from national pharmacy organizations, including NABP, regarding the actions planned or taken by these national pharmacy organizations related to the oversight of drug compounding.

We conducted this performance audit from February 2013 to July 2013 in accordance with generally accepted government auditing standards. Those standards require that we plan and perform the audit to obtain sufficient, appropriate evidence to provide a reasonable basis for our findings and conclusions based on our audit objectives. We believe that the evidence obtained provides a reasonable basis for our findings and conclusions based on our audit objectives.

Background

Drug Compounding by Pharmacies

Traditionally, a drug is compounded, through the process of mixing, combining, or altering ingredients, to create a customized drug tailored to the medical needs of an individual patient upon receipt of a prescription. For example, a pharmacist may tailor a drug for a patient who is allergic to an ingredient in a manufactured drug or prepare a liquid formulation for a patient who has difficulty swallowing pills. Some pharmacies also compound drugs in advance of receiving individual patient prescriptions in anticipation of receiving prescriptions based on historical prescribing patterns, a practice referred to as anticipatory compounding. Compounded drugs include nonsterile preparations, such as capsules, ointments, creams, gels, and suppositories; and sterile preparations, including intravenously administered fluids and injectable drugs. Compounded sterile drugs pose special risks of contamination if not made properly and require special safeguards to prevent injury or death to patients receiving them.

Drug compounding is an integral part of the pharmacy profession and is practiced in a variety of settings, including hospital pharmacies, community pharmacies, chain drug store pharmacies, and home infusion settings. The exact proportion of all prescriptions filled by compounded drugs is unknown. In 2003, we reported that estimates ranged from 1 percent to 10 percent.[9] More recently, in 2013, the International Academy of Compounding Pharmacists estimated that the compounding industry made up 1 to 3 percent of the U.S. prescription drug market.

The exact number of pharmacies that compound drugs is also unknown. In 2013, the International Academy of Compounding Pharmacists provided the following estimates:

- About 26,000 community-based pharmacies reported that they provide some sort of prescription compounding services, based on information from the National Council of Prescription Drug Program's database on pharmacies.

- Of those 26,000 community-based pharmacies, about 7,500 pharmacies specialize in compounding.

- Of those 7,500 community-based pharmacies that specialize in compounding, about 3,000 pharmacies compound both sterile and nonsterile preparations.

- In addition, there are about 8,200 hospital pharmacies in the United States, and all of them are likely conducting some sort of compounding, both sterile and nonsterile.

---

[9]GAO-04-195T.

A recent report indicates that there has been an increase in the outsourcing of drug compounding in the last decade, primarily by hospitals. In April 2013, the HHS-OIG reported that nearly all (92 percent) of surveyed hospitals that participated in Medicare reported using compounded sterile products, and that more than three-fourths of these hospitals (77 percent) purchased some of these compounded drugs from at least one outside pharmacy.[10] The HHS-OIG found factors that hospitals cited for outsourcing included the need to ensure a ready supply of products in the event of shortages and the need for products with extended shelf lives, which require sophisticated equipment and testing to prepare these products that may not be readily available on the hospital premises.

State Regulation of Pharmacy Practice

State pharmacy regulatory bodies are responsible for oversight of the practice of pharmacy. All 50 states describe drug compounding in their state laws and regulations on pharmacy practice, although specific statutes or regulations vary across states, according to NABP.

USP is involved in setting standards that affect compounding.[11] According to USP, compounding standards help practitioners adhere to widely acknowledged, scientifically sound procedures and best practices, and facilitate the delivery of consistent and good-quality prepared medicines to patients. Twenty-five state pharmacy regulatory bodies reported that

---

[10]Department of Health and Human Services, Office of Inspector General, *High-Risk Compounded Sterile Preparations and Outsourcing by Hospitals That Use Them* (Washington, D.C.: Apr. 10, 2013).

[11]USP's current suite of General Chapters for compounding includes: Chapter 797 Pharmaceutical Compounding—Sterile Preparations, which provides procedures and requirements for compounding sterile preparations; Chapter 795 Pharmaceutical Compounding—Nonsterile Preparations, which provides guidance on applying good compounding practices in the preparation of nonsterile compounded formulations for dispensing and/or administration to humans or animals; Chapter 1160—Pharmaceutical Calculations in Prescription Compounding; Chapter 1163—Quality Assurance in Pharmaceutical Compounding; and Chapter 1176—Prescription Balances and Volumetric Apparatus. According to USP officials, these compounding chapters reference an additional 48 USP chapters. In addition to setting standards that affect compounding, USP, through the *United States Pharmacopeia-National Formulary*, a compendium of public pharmacopeial standards, provides monographs for drug articles, including ingredients used in compounded preparations, and monographs for the compounded preparations themselves, comprising standards of identity, quality, purity, strength, packaging, and labeling.

they require compliance with USP's chapter on sterile compounding, according to the NABP's 2013 survey of pharmacy law.[12]

FDA Regulation of Drug Compounding

FDA considers compounded drugs to be "new drugs" subject to FDA oversight; however, the agency has acknowledged that it is not practicable for pharmacies to complete and obtain approval for a new drug application for each compounded drug prepared for an individual patient.[13] In 1992, FDA, through guidance, and, in 1997, Congress, through legislation, attempted to clarify when compounded drugs will be exempt from certain requirements of the FDCA, including new drug approval requirements. Specifically, the Food and Drug Administration Modernization Act of 1997 (FDAMA) enacted section 503A of the FDCA. This section exempted drug products compounded by a pharmacist or physician based on a valid prescription for a compounded product that is necessary for the identified patient from three key provisions of the FDCA that are otherwise applicable to drugs, provided the pharmacy had, among other conditions, not solicited prescriptions or advertised or promoted the compounded drugs.[14]

In 2001, however, the United States Court of Appeals for the Ninth Circuit struck down all of the advertising, promotion, and solicitation provisions of section 503A of the FDCA because those provisions violated the Free

---

[12]National Association of Boards of Pharmacy, *Survey of Pharmacy Law—2013* (Mount Prospect, IL: 2013). The pharmacy regulatory bodies of Guam and Puerto Rico also reported that they require compliance with USP's standards on sterile compounding.

[13]The FDCA defines "new drug" as "Any drug ... the composition of which is such that such drug is not generally recognized, among experts qualified by scientific training and experience to evaluate the safety and effectiveness of drugs, as safe and effective for use under the conditions prescribed, recommended, or suggested in the labeling thereof. . . . ." 21 U.S.C. § 321(p)(1). Drug manufacturers submit new drug applications to FDA to seek approval to market and sell a new pharmaceutical drug product in the United States. In addition, abbreviated new drug applications are submitted to FDA to seek approval to market a generic version of a drug after the period of exclusivity and any patents for a brand-name drug expire. In fiscal year 2013, user fees for new drug applications ranged from $979,400 to $1,958,800, depending on whether or not the application required clinical data, and were $51,520 for abbreviated new drug applications.

[14]Pub. L. No. 105-115, § 127, 111 Stat. 2296, 2328 (Nov. 21, 1997). Compounded drug products that met these requirements did not have to comply with good manufacturing practices, label drugs with adequate directions for use, or have an FDA-approved new drug or abbreviated new drug application. References to section 503A in this report are to section 503A of the FDCA, as codified at 21 U.S.C. § 353a.

Speech Clause of the First Amendment. The court also held that, because these provisions could not be severed from the remainder of section 503A, all of section 503A was invalid. In 2002, the United States Supreme Court struck down the law's advertising, promotion, and solicitation restrictions without addressing whether the rest of section 503A remained law. As a result, FDA issued a revised version of its compliance policy guide on drug compounding in 2002, which provides guidance, in light of the Ninth Circuit and Supreme Court decisions, on the types of factors the agency will consider in determining whether to take enforcement action against drug compounders for violations of the FDCA. These factors include activities, such as offering compounded drug products at wholesale, that suggest a drug compounder is engaged in drug manufacturing, rather than drug compounding. Subsequently, in 2005, the United States Court of Appeals for the Fifth Circuit issued a decision holding that, although section 503A's advertising, promotion, and solicitation restrictions were invalid, these restrictions could be severed from the rest of section 503A and, therefore, the law's remaining drug compounding provisions remain valid. See appendix II for details about these developments and how they have affected FDA's authority to oversee drug compounding.

The FDCA provides FDA authority to inspect pharmacies that compound drugs; however, this authority is limited. Generally, FDA's inspection authority does not extend to a pharmacy's records if the pharmacy meets certain requirements.[15] While FDA has not routinely inspected compounding pharmacies, FDA has used its authority to conduct some inspections in recent years, generally in response to complaints. These inspections have resulted in FDA issuing inspection observation reports, which are called FDA form 483s, and, in some cases, warning letters.[16] FDA's FACTS database contains information on these inspections,

---

[15]A pharmacy's records are exempt from FDA's inspection authority if the pharmacy is in compliance with any applicable local laws regulating the practice of pharmacy and medicine, regularly engages in dispensing drugs upon a prescription from a licensed practitioner, and does not manufacture, prepare, or compound drugs for sale other than during the regular course of its business of dispensing or selling drugs at retail. 21 U.S.C. § 374(a)(2)(A).

[16]An FDA form 483 is an inspection observation report that lists objectionable conditions observed at the facilities. An FDA warning letter is a correspondence that notifies a responsible individual or firm that the agency considers one or more products, practices, processes, or other activities to be in violation of the FDCA, its implementing regulations, and other federal statutes.

including the type of inspection (e.g., routine or in response to a complaint).

Under the FDCA, drug manufacturers are required to register with FDA and list the drugs they manufacture.[17] The FDCA exempts from these registration and listing requirements those pharmacies that meet certain requirements.[18] FDA's Drug Registration and Listing System contains information on drug establishments that have registered with FDA to market their drugs in the United States. These establishments provide information, including company name and address, and identify the drugs they manufacture for commercial distribution in the United States.

Unclear Federal Authority and Lack of Consensus on When Drug Compounding Becomes Manufacturing

Although FDAMA attempted to clarify FDA's authority to oversee drug compounding, subsequent court decisions have contributed to a lack of clarity regarding the legal standards FDA must apply to oversee drug compounding. Specifically, two federal circuit court decisions resulted in differing FDA authority over drug compounding in different parts of the country, which has affected FDA's ability to oversee drug compounding. Section 503A provisions exempting certain compounded drugs from the FDCA's good manufacturing practice, certain labeling, and new drug and abbreviated new drug application requirements are in effect in those states in the Fifth Circuit, in which the U.S. Court of Appeals has held that the law, other than its advertising, promotion, and solicitation provisions, is valid. However, FDA follows its 2002 compliance policy guide in states in the Ninth Circuit, in which the U.S. Court of Appeals has held all of the drug compounding provisions in section 503A are invalid. In states outside of the Fifth and Ninth Circuits, where federal courts have not considered the validity of these drug compounding provisions, FDA considers both section 503A's drug compounding provisions and its 2002 compliance policy guide to guide its oversight. Figure 1 shows how FDA generally conducts its oversight of drug compounding in different parts of the country based on the differing court decisions.

---

[17]21 U.S.C. § 360.

[18]A pharmacy is exempt from these registration and listing requirements if the pharmacy is in compliance with any applicable local laws regulating the practice of pharmacy and medicine, regularly engages in dispensing drugs upon a prescription from a licensed practitioner, and does not manufacture, prepare, or compound drugs for sale other than during the regular course of its business of dispensing or selling drugs at retail. 21 U.S.C. § 360(g)(1).

Figure 1: Food and Drug Administration (FDA) Oversight of Drug Compounding

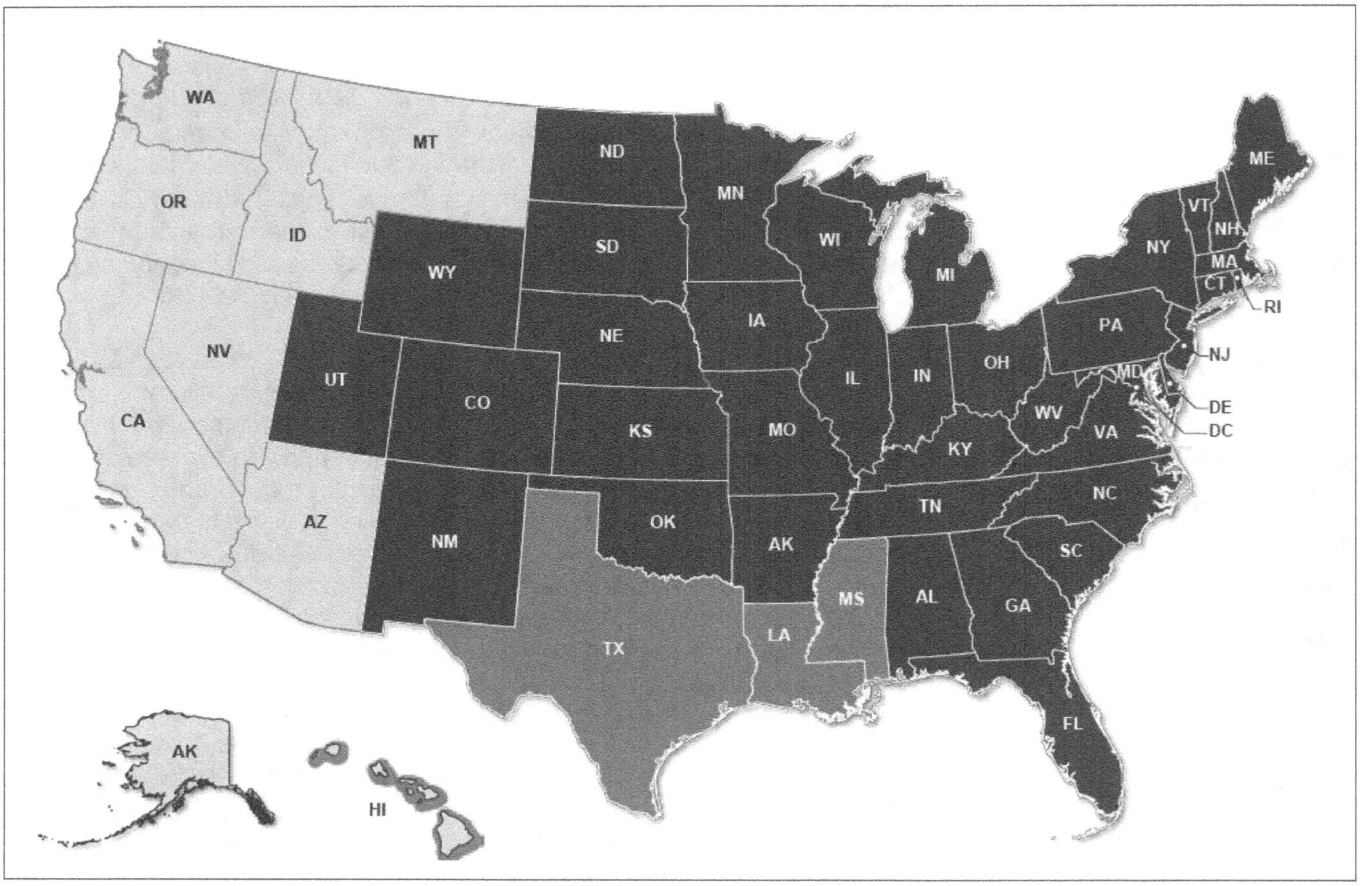

Interactive instructions

Roll over he color legend to the right for information about FDA's authority to oversee drug compounding and how it approaches oversight of these drugs.

Area/Jurisdiction affected

Ninth Circuit   Fifth Circuit   Remaining states

Sources: GAO analysis of federal court decisions and interviews with FDA officials; Map Resources (map).

Furthermore, according to FDA officials, the agency's inconsistent authority to oversee drug compounding and the agency's limited inspection authority over pharmacies have led to legal challenges to FDA's authority to inspect entities engaging in drug compounding and to take appropriate enforcement actions against these entities. For example, from 2002 through 2012, FDA had to obtain 11 inspection warrants to gain access to drug compounders' facilities and records, representing nearly half of the 25 administrative warrants obtained by FDA for all FDA-regulated products in that same period, according to agency officials.[19] FDA officials said that these entities refused FDA access to their facilities or records, citing the provision of the FDCA that limits the agency's inspection authority over a pharmacy that is in compliance with state and local laws.[20] FDA officials added that if the agency is required to obtain a warrant before gaining access, the agency may be delayed in its efforts to curb an outbreak or take enforcement action and the entity may have time to clean up its facility or alter its records to avoid enforcement action. FDA officials also said that if the agency finds significant issues during an inspection of a drug compounder, to determine whether to take action against the compounder the agency must first consider its legal authority in the particular jurisdiction in which the compounder operates and whether any FDA action is likely to be challenged in court. According to FDA officials, engaging in this type of analysis may have resulted in a long lag time between the inspection and the issuance of a warning letter.

In addition, we found a lack of consensus regarding when drug compounding becomes drug manufacturing. Officials from FDA and national pharmacy organizations we interviewed generally agreed that traditional drug compounding involves a patient-specific prescription for a customized medication that is not otherwise commercially available, and there was agreement that this type of compounding is part of the practice of pharmacy and generally overseen by the states. Further, there was agreement that FDA has clear authority to oversee drug manufacturing and drug manufacturers. However, there was not agreement on whether compounding pharmacies that are engaged in large-scale drug

---

[19]According to FDA officials, the agency typically seeks inspection warrants when inspection has been refused completely or when refusals have been encountered in limited areas (e.g., when a firm has refused to allow FDA to take photographs or collect samples). FDA officials also reported having to obtain warrants to inspect 2 of 31 compounding pharmacies it inspected in 2013.

[20]21 U.S.C. § 374(a)(2)(A).

compounding, producing these drugs in anticipation of individual prescriptions or without prescriptions, and selling them across state lines, are engaged in the practice of pharmacy or are engaged in drug manufacturing. As a result, there is a lack of consensus regarding whether states should have primary responsibility for regulating these entities as pharmacies, or FDA should have primary responsibility to regulate them as manufacturers. This lack of consensus on who has primary responsibility to regulate entities engaged in these practices and differing FDA authority applicable to compounded drugs across the country has resulted in gaps in oversight of drug compounding.

Further, according to officials from FDA and most of the organizations we spoke with, the line is not clear when anticipatory compounding is part of the practice of pharmacy and when anticipatory compounding crosses into drug manufacturing. For example, officials from one national pharmacy organization said that if a certain number of patients come to a pharmacy every month for progesterone suppositories and the pharmacy makes enough for a month's supply in advance based on the history of these prescriptions, then a pharmacy's compounding of the drug in advance should be considered drug compounding and not manufacturing. However, these officials added that a pharmacy that makes 10,000 sterile compounded injectables in advance of a prescription and ships them across 18 states may be engaged in manufacturing.

Noting this lack of clarity regarding when drug compounding becomes manufacturing, FDA has been working on a proposal that would create a new category of "nontraditional compounding," which would be subject to FDA oversight. According to congressional testimony and public statements,[21] FDA's new category of "nontraditional drug compounders" would fall between traditional drug compounding and drug manufacturing. FDA officials said they believe this new category would subject entities with a higher potential to adversely affect a large number of patients to appropriate and effective FDA regulation and oversight. FDA's proposal describes an entity as engaging in nontraditional compounding if it produces sterile compounded products in advance of or without an individual patient prescription, and ships these sterile compounded products across state lines. Under FDA's proposal, state pharmacy

---

[21]For example, Statement of Janet Woodcock, M.D., Director, Center for Drug Evaluation and Research, FDA, before the Senate Committee on Health, Education, Labor, and Pensions, 113th Cong., May 9, 2013.

regulatory bodies would continue to have primary responsibility to oversee traditional drug compounding and FDA would have express statutory authority to oversee this new category of nontraditional drug compounding.[22]

Some national pharmacy organizations said that the creation of a new category of nontraditional drug compounding is not necessary because they believe drug compounding and drug manufacturing are already distinct. For example, officials from one national pharmacy organization we interviewed said the establishment of a new category of nontraditional drug compounding could create more confusion between drug compounding and manufacturing, unless this new category is carefully crafted. These officials said that states should regulate drug compounding and FDA should regulate drug manufacturing, and that once an entity crosses the line between drug compounding and manufacturing, there should be a seamless handoff from the state to FDA. However, other organizations we spoke with generally agreed with FDA's proposed tiered system and said that entities in this new category should be regulated by FDA, not by state pharmacy regulatory bodies.

FDA Lacks Reliable and Timely Data on Compounding Pharmacies, but Has Found Problems through Its Limited Oversight

FDA lacks reliable information on entities that compound drugs, the types of drugs being compounded, and adverse events related to compounded drugs. Until 2013, FDA limited its inspections of compounding pharmacies to those conducted in response to complaints or adverse events, called "for cause" inspections; however, the agency has recently conducted inspections of compounding pharmacies that were known to produce "high-risk" sterile compounded drugs, and identified serious problems.

---

[22]On June 19, 2013, the Senate Committee on Health, Education, Labor and Pensions reported out of committee a bill that would create a new category of "compounding manufacturer," which is similar in some respects to FDA's proposed category of "nontraditional drug compounder." Pharmaceutical Compounding Quality and Accountability Act, S. 959, 113th Cong. (1st Sess. 2013). In addition, on May 23, 2013, a bill was introduced in the House of Representatives, H.R. 2186, to strengthen federal oversight of drug compounding. VALID Compounding Act, H.R. 2186, 113th Cong. (1st. Sess. 2013).

FDA Has Not Collected Reliable and Timely Data on Compounded Drugs and the Entities That Prepare Them

FDA officials, including the FDA Commissioner, have stated that, under the FDCA, compounding pharmacies are generally not required to register with FDA or list their products, and therefore FDA does not know who they are and what they are compounding.[23] As a result, FDA has stated that one of the reasons it has not routinely inspected compounding pharmacies is because the agency does not know who they are.

Officials with some of the organizations we interviewed said there has been confusion regarding the extent to which FDA oversees the compounding pharmacies that registered with FDA as drug manufacturers. Although drug manufacturers are required to register with FDA by providing company information such as name, location, and the drugs the company manufactures, compounding pharmacies meeting the FDCA's registration exemption are not required to register. However, according to FDA officials, neither the law nor the agency precludes those compounding pharmacies that are exempt from registration from voluntarily doing so, and some compounding pharmacies have registered with FDA as manufacturers and marketed themselves as "FDA-registered." FDA officials told us that registering as a manufacturer does not necessarily result in the application of regulatory requirements that apply to manufacturers or in FDA inspection for compliance with these requirements. For example, a compounding pharmacy may voluntarily register with FDA; however, this registration does not by itself give FDA authority to require the pharmacy to comply with FDA's good manufacturing practices and other requirements that apply to drug manufacturers. Nonetheless, these pharmacies appear as registered manufacturers in FDA's registration database, the Drug Registration and Listing System.

When entities that compound drugs on a large scale register with FDA as manufacturers and market themselves as "FDA-registered," it may erroneously convey an endorsement by FDA. As a result, some state officials and purchasers may incorrectly assume FDA inspects the entities or has reviewed and approved their compounded drugs. Officials from one of the national pharmacy organizations told us that they recently

---

[23]Pharmacies are not required to register with FDA if they follow any applicable local laws regulating the practice of pharmacy and medicine, regularly engage in dispensing drugs upon a prescription from a licensed practitioner, and do not manufacture, prepare, or compound drugs for sale other than during the regular course of their business of dispensing or selling drugs at retail. 21 U.S.C. § 360(g)(1).

learned that a pharmacy can be registered with FDA as a drug establishment as well as with the state as a pharmacy. They added that healthcare professionals and the public may assume that if an entity registers with FDA then that means that FDA is in some way regulating that entity. In addition, NABP officials noted that they were aware of some entities engaged in drug compounding whose drug compounding activities are not subject to state oversight because they are registered as manufacturers with FDA and the states assume FDA is overseeing these activities. Yet, if a compounding pharmacy is voluntarily registered with FDA, the agency would not inspect it for compliance with good manufacturing practices because it does not manufacture FDA-approved drugs.

Further, FDA lacks reliable data to make decisions to prioritize its inspection workload and other follow-up and enforcement actions.[24] Under standards for internal control in the federal government, relevant, reliable, and timely information should be available for external reporting purposes and management decision making. According to FDA officials, although the agency's FACTS database has a code for inspections of compounding facilities, some compounding pharmacies could be inspected and coded as either manufacturers of human drugs or manufacturers of veterinary drugs, and the FACTS database would not identify them as inspections of compounding pharmacies. In addition, while FDA can manually look up the results of an individual inspection, the agency does not have ready access to all of the final classification of inspections for those compounding pharmacies it can identify in its FACTS database; in these instances, FACTS does not indicate the agency's final determination whether an official action was indicated, voluntary action was indicated, or if no action was indicated from the inspection results.[25] According to FDA officials, some of the final

---

[24]We have previously reported on weaknesses in the data FDA uses to prioritize its inspection workload, including FACTS. See, for example, GAO, *Drug Safety: Better Data Management and More Inspections Are Needed to Strengthen FDA's Foreign Drug Inspection Program*, GAO-08-970 (Washington, D.C.: Sept. 22, 2008).

[25]FDA classifies an inspection as "official action indicated" if objectionable conditions were found that warrant regulatory action by the agency. A classification of "voluntary action indicated" means that objectionable conditions were identified but any corrective actions are left to the establishment to take voluntarily. A classification of "no action indicated" means that no objectionable conditions or practices were found during the inspection (i.e., conditions or practices that violate current good manufacturing practices), or if the significance of the documented objectionable conditions found does not justify further FDA action.

decisions are in hard copy, and the database includes recommendations from the district office inspectors, which may differ from the final inspection classifications.[26] Without reliable, timely data on all inspections conducted and the actions required and taken following those inspections, FDA lacks ready access to key data to inform its decision making on its oversight priorities and to take appropriate action when problems are identified.

In addition, pharmacies are generally not required to report to FDA adverse events regarding compounded drugs they have produced, unlike drug manufacturers who are required to report to FDA if they become aware of adverse events associated with their products.[27] Therefore, adverse event data about compounded drugs consists of voluntary reports, and FDA officials said that the agency is only aware that an adverse event involves a compounded drug if the individual voluntarily reporting the adverse event specifies that a compounded drug was involved in the event. While FDA's adverse event data associated with compounded drugs is limited, a recent report by the Pew Charitable Trusts identified 20 pharmacy compounding errors associated with 1,022 adverse events, including 75 deaths, since 2001.[28] According to this report, contamination of sterile products was the most common compounding error, though some incidents were the result of

---

[26]According to FDA officials, the agency does not have ready access to all of the final inspection classifications as some of the records are in hard copy and it would be difficult and time consuming to review the inspection reports and any associated documentation to evaluate and determine why certain final decisions were made or not made. Agency officials told us that reasons why a final decision was not entered into its FACTS database include, but are not limited to, the difficulty of the agency to come to a final classification determination on an inspection due to the complexity of legal issues associated with the regulation of compounded drugs and compounding pharmacies or failure to enter the data.

[27]Generally, if a manufacturer receives drug- or certain device-related adverse event reports, it must send them to FDA. Health care professionals and consumers can voluntarily file adverse event reports with FDA and may also report these events to the products' manufacturers. User facilities (e.g., hospitals and nursing homes) must report certain device-related—but not drug-related—adverse events to FDA as well. 21 C.F.R. §§ 314.80(c), 803.30, 803.50.

[28]The Pew Charitable Trusts is an independent, nonprofit research and public policy organization. Pew Charitable Trusts, American Society of Health-System Pharmacists, American Hospital Association, *Pharmacy Sterile Compounding Summit: Summary of a Stakeholder Meeting* (Washington D.C.: Apr. 15, 2013).

pharmacists' and technicians' miscalculations and mistakes in filling prescriptions.

Oversight of Drug Compounders Has Been Limited, but FDA Has Recently Increased Its Efforts

Until 2013, FDA limited its inspections of compounding pharmacies to those conducted in response to complaints or adverse events, called "for cause" inspections;[29] however, the agency has recently conducted inspections of compounding pharmacies that FDA identified as known to produce "high-risk" sterile compounded drugs. From its available data, FDA identified 194 "for cause" inspections of compounding pharmacies the agency conducted from February 8, 2002, through May 11, 2012, under its pharmacy compounding assignment code for human drugs.[30] Of these 194 inspections, FDA issued 63 form 483 inspection observation reports outlining significant objectionable conditions identified during the inspections. FDA subsequently issued at least 31 warning letters to pharmacies as a result of these inspections for problems such as bacterial and fungal contamination found in sterile clean rooms and in finished product samples, improper hygiene and garbing procedures (e.g., putting on gowns, gloves, and shoe covers), failure to conduct appropriate laboratory testing on drug products, and inadequate ventilation. However, FDA has not taken any enforcement actions against the 31 entities where the agency found problems significant enough to send warning letters, according to FDA officials. Further, we found that 19 of the 194 compounding pharmacies were registered with FDA as drug manufacturers.

While FDA policy requires that the final inspection classification (which states whether official action, voluntary action, or no action was indicated based on the inspection findings) be entered into the agency's FACTS database, FDA officials said they could not readily provide the final

---

[29]FDA's inspection plan for fiscal year 2011 called for five full-time equivalent staff to inspect compounding pharmacies, and its plan for fiscal year 2012 called for two full-time equivalent investigator staff for these inspections.

[30]FDA officials noted that this is likely an incomplete list of inspections of compounding pharmacies. That is, they said that the agency could have conducted additional inspections of compounding pharmacies; but they could only identify 194 of them because of limitations in FDA's inspections database. According to FDA officials, additional inspections may have been coded as investigations rather than inspections (although they involved inspectional activity as part of the investigation) and some inspections of compounding pharmacies could have been coded as inspections of human drug manufacturers.

inspection classification for the 194 inspections of compounding pharmacies. The officials said that in some cases the database included FDA district officials' recommendations for inspection classification rather than the final inspection classification. As a result, we could not ascertain how many of the 194 inspections of compounding pharmacies found problems that were significant enough for FDA to determine that official action was indicated.

More recently, FDA began inspecting compounding pharmacies in February 2013 that, according to the agency, were known to produce "high-risk" sterile compounded drugs.[31] These inspections were not the for-cause inspections that FDA has typically done in the past when inspecting compounding pharmacies. Rather, FDA's objective was to determine whether certain pharmacies that were known to have produced high-risk sterile drug products in the past posed a significant threat to public health from poor production practices. According to FDA officials, the agency identified 31 compounding pharmacies to inspect using criteria that included whether a warning letter had been issued to the pharmacy in the past 10 years, whether the pharmacy compounded sterile injectable drugs, whether there were adverse drug events reported, or whether there were complaints received from the FDA district office or others. FDA officials said they also reviewed related congressional committee reports that mentioned specific pharmacies and reviewed pharmacy websites. In summarizing these efforts, FDA reported that pharmacies meeting at least two of FDA's criteria were included in the inspections.[32]

As of April 29, 2013, FDA had issued form 483 inspection observation reports to 30 of the 31 compounding pharmacies it inspected as part of its

---

[31]For FDA's summary describing these inspections, see Food and Drug Administration, *Summary: 2013 FDA Pharmacy Inspection Assignment*, accessed April 30, 2013, http://www.fda.gov/Drugs/GuidanceComplianceRegulatoryInformation/PharmacyCompounding/ucm347722.htm. FDA officials told us that to conduct these inspections of compounding pharmacies the agency had to take inspectors off other assignments.

[32]According to FDA officials, the agency used a risk-based model to identify the pharmacies and 15 of the 31 pharmacies had at least one reported death and, thus, were included in FDA's inspections regardless of whether they met any of the other criteria.

recent inspections.[33] FDA's observations included inappropriate or inadequate, or both, clothing for sterile processing, lack of appropriate air filtration systems, insufficient microbiological testing, and other practices that create risk of contamination.

As of May 21, 2013, 7 of the 31 compounding pharmacies had voluntarily recalled some or all of their sterile compounded products as a result of observations from these recent FDA inspections.[34] For example:

- FDA sampled a compounded sterile injectable solution during one of its inspections in March 2013 and found bacteria in the product, which resulted in the compounding pharmacy immediately announcing a nationwide recall of all of its sterile compounded products, which included over 50 sterile drug products.

- Another compounding pharmacy recalled its sterile drug products that had not yet reached the expiration date listed on the product because of a lack of sterility assurance. This recall included approximately 95 dosage units of various sterile compounded drugs that the pharmacy supplied to the offices of licensed medical professionals located within its state; however, some patients that received products from those medical professionals may live in other states.

Further, according to our analysis, 10 of the 31 high-risk compounding pharmacies that FDA inspected were also registered in FDA's drug manufacturer database. Even though these compounding pharmacies were registered with FDA, agency officials said the agency does not routinely inspect these pharmacies despite their registration because registration alone does not trigger a routine inspection. Additionally, 8 of the 10 were individual facilities of two different larger compounding

---

[33]According to FDA officials, 1 of the 31 pharmacies the agency inspected did not receive an FDA form 483, and this pharmacy was not compounding sterile drugs. Four of the 31 pharmacies were individual facilities of one pharmacy firm, and 4 others were individual facilities of another firm; however, FDA counted each facility as a separate compounding pharmacy.

[34]In addition, as of May 30, 2013, four other compounding pharmacies that were not part of the 31 pharmacies inspected by FDA initiated voluntary recalls of their sterile compounded products because of concerns of a lack of sterility assurance. FDA identified bacterial and fungal growth in samples of a sterile compounded drug in a subsequent inspection of one of these compounding pharmacies.

pharmacies, both of which had websites advertising they were FDA-registered.

States and National Organizations Have Taken Various Actions to Strengthen Oversight of Drug Compounding

The four states we reviewed—California, Connecticut, Florida, and Iowa—have each recently taken actions, such as working with national pharmacy organizations, to improve their oversight of drug compounding. In addition, national pharmacy organizations have undertaken efforts to help states oversee drug compounding. However, some states may lack the resources to provide the necessary oversight of drug compounding.

The Four States Reviewed Have Taken Actions, Including Increased Inspections, to Strengthen Oversight of Drug Compounding

All four of the states we reviewed recently took steps to potentially strengthen their oversight of drug compounding. These steps included developing an inspection program for sterile drug compounders that dispense drugs in the state, but are located outside of the state, and drafting new legislation to require the board of pharmacy to conduct on-site inspections prior to licensing a pharmacy. Examples of actions taken by each of the four states we reviewed follow:

California: On May 29, 2013, the California Senate passed legislation that would prohibit any pharmacy from compounding or dispensing, and any nonresident pharmacy from compounding for shipping into the state, sterile compounded drug products unless the pharmacy has obtained a sterile compounding pharmacy license from the California Board of Pharmacy; require inspection of resident and nonresident pharmacies by the board prior to licensure; require resident and nonresident pharmacies to report adverse events for compounded drugs to both the California State Board of Pharmacy and MedWatch, FDA's adverse event reporting system; and require resident and nonresident pharmacies to submit a list of all sterile medications compounded by the pharmacy during the prior 12 months before obtaining an annual renewal of the sterile compounding license, among other requirements. Currently, California law requires that a pharmacy that compounds sterile injectable drug products in California, or that ships sterile injectable products into California, obtain a special license issued by the board; however, the law exempts from this licensure requirement certain pharmacies that have current accreditation from a private accreditation agency approved by the board.[35] California pharmacies that obtain licensure by the board are subject to prelicensure inspections, as well as annual inspections prior to renewal of the license. Nonresident pharmacies must provide a copy of a recent inspection report issued by the pharmacy's licensing agency, or a recent report from a private accrediting agency approved by the board, documenting the pharmacy's compliance with board regulations regarding the compounding of injectable sterile drug products. In describing the board's support of the proposed legislation, a California State Board of Pharmacy official told us that the board believed it important that all California and nonresident pharmacies compounding sterile injectable drugs be subject to state inspections, including those with an accreditation. As of June 14, 2013, the legislation was pending before a California State Assembly committee.

Connecticut: An official from Connecticut's Drug Control Division—which conducts inspections of pharmacies in the state and houses the Commission of Pharmacy Board Administrator, which oversees pharmacy licensing—told us that, as of April 2013, the state was working to tighten its regulations and implement inspection practices regarding in-state sterile drug compounders. For example, the state plans to begin conducting more thorough pharmacy inspections in which the inspectors consider additional attributes, such as compliance with USP standards on sterile compounding, the physical environment where the facility is located, and the number of sales representatives employed by the pharmacy. In addition, the Drug Control Division is working to propose new regulations to allow the state to better track and regulate the sale of compounded sterile medications produced by resident and nonresident

---

[35]Resident pharmacies operated by entities that are licensed by either the board or the California Department of Health and nonresident pharmacies operated by entities that are licensed as a hospital, home health agency, or a skilled nursing facility are eligble for such exemption. Cal. Bus. & Prof. Code §§ 4127.1, 4127.2. In contrast to current law, which imposes special licensure requirements only on pharmacies compounding injectable sterile drugs, the proposed legislation would require pharmacies compounding all types of sterile drugs to meet such requirements.

sterile drug compounders. However, the details of these proposed regulations were not available as of June 2013.[36]

Florida: On November 20, 2012, the Florida Board of Pharmacy issued an emergency rule requiring all resident pharmacies and nonresident pharmacies that ship drugs to Florida to immediately notify the board of their compounding activities.[37] More than half (55 percent) of the 8,193 responding pharmacies reported that they compound nonsterile products, such as ointments or tablets; and 12 percent reported that they compound sterile products, such as injectable and ophthalmic solutions. Florida found that about one-third (32 percent) of the 946 pharmacies that perform sterile compounding were nonresident pharmacies.[38] One goal of Florida's emergency rule was to determine the scope of sterile and nonsterile compounding within Florida's resident and nonresident licensed pharmacies. According to Florida Board of Pharmacy officials, prior to the emergency rule, the board did not know how many pharmacies compounded drugs, how many nonresident pharmacies shipped compounded drugs into the state, or whether they compounded nonsterile or sterile drugs. According to these officials, the board intends to use this newly acquired information to improve the board's oversight activities, such as to identify and inspect compounding pharmacies. As of May 2013, the Florida Board of Pharmacy was considering whether to

---

[36]In Connecticut, pharmacy licensure and pharmacy inspections are handled separately. The state's Commission of Pharmacy, which is administered by the Department of Consumer Protection, is responsible for approval of new licenses. The commission also adjudicates cases involving pharmacists, pharmacies, and pharmacy technicians brought before it. The Department of Consumer Protection's Licensing Division handles the clerical aspects of licensing pharmacists and pharmacies while the state's Department of Consumer Protection, Drug Control Division, conducts pharmacy inspections and implements enforcement actions. Connecticut has 10 drug control agents who conduct pharmacy inspections, all of whom are licensed pharmacists.

[37]Specifically, Florida's emergency rule required resident pharmacies with state pharmacy permits and nonresident pharmacies registered with the state to immediately notify the board of their sterile and nonsterile compounding activities, the types of drugs they compound, and whether they compound drugs in bu k. In addition, the emergency rule required Florida's board of pharmacy to use the information on compounding activities to place a high priority on inspecting high-risk pharmacies such as those that compound sterile drugs. The emergency rule also required all nonresident registered pharmacies to provide a copy of their last two inspection reports as provided by the state in which the pharmacies are physically located and licensed.

[38]Florida Department of Health, Division of Medical Quality Assurance, *Florida Board of Pharmacy Compounding Survey Report* (Tallahassee, FL: Jan. 23, 2013).

require pharmacies to complete an updated survey biennially in order to renew their pharmacy licenses.

Iowa: Iowa is inspecting drug compounders that are licensed by the state as nonresident pharmacies and dispensing compounded drugs in Iowa. Iowa established a consultancy services agreement with NABP in December 2012, and inspectors from NABP began inspecting the 581 nonresident pharmacies identified by the state at that time. The results of these inspections are expected to reveal whether the selected pharmacies are compounding drugs in compliance with state regulations. According to Iowa Board of Pharmacy officials, the state does not have information on the extent that Iowa's licensed nonresident pharmacies compound drugs, how many nonresident pharmacies ship compounded drugs into the state, or whether they compound nonsterile or sterile drugs. However, NABP's inspections have begun to provide some of this information. As of April 2013, Iowa's Board of Pharmacy had taken six formal disciplinary actions against five out-of-state compounding pharmacies following NABP inspections and, according to an Iowa Board of Pharmacy official, the board anticipates more disciplinary actions during the remainder of 2013 and early 2014. By the end of 2013 or early in 2014, an Iowa Board of Pharmacy official anticipates that NABP inspectors would visit all nonresident pharmacies licensed by the state.

States May Leverage National Organizations' Efforts to Enhance Oversight of Drug Compounding

At the national level, pharmacy organizations have undertaken a number of efforts to help states oversee drug compounding. For example, national pharmacy organizations have developed standards for compounded drugs that could be adopted by states. The following are examples of efforts undertaken by national pharmacy organizations.

The National Association of Boards of Pharmacy (NABP): NABP has initiated the Compounding Action Plan to identify and inspect compounding pharmacies. It includes continued collaboration on the Iowa nonresident inspection program, discussed above, and the sharing of inspection results and related actions. Through this plan, NABP intends to collect data on the number of compounding pharmacies, including their scope of operations, in all states, and inspect these pharmacies. NABP officials said they believe that many of the 581 nonresident pharmacies licensed and identified by the Iowa Board of Pharmacy also hold licenses with many, if not all, of the other states requiring nonresident licensure. Using the Iowa nonresident licensed pharmacy list as a starting point, NABP sent Iowa's list to each state to confirm information regarding these pharmacies, such as whether the pharmacy has been disciplined, whether it is engaged in sterile compounding, or whether it is engaged in "nontraditional" compounding activities. In addition, NABP asked all states to identify any known or suspected compounding pharmacies in their state that are not on the Iowa nonresident pharmacy list. As a result, NABP officials told us that NABP added some additional pharmacies to Iowa's original inspection list. As of June 2013, NABP had inspected 215 pharmacies.[39] In addition to its Compounding Action Plan, NABP created and continues to maintain a Model State Pharmacy Act and Model Rules for states to use when developing new pharmacy laws and regulations, including rules specific to sterile compounding. According to NABP officials, each state has adopted aspects of NABP's model act and model rules.[40]

The Pharmacy Compounding Accreditation Board (PCAB): In 2006, eight national pharmacy organizations established the PCAB, a voluntary accrediting organization for sterile and nonsterile drug compounders.[41] According to an organization official, PCAB's national standards are based on the consensus of industry experts of those elements that should exist in a pharmacy that adheres to high quality standards. PCAB accreditation indicates that the staff involved in compounding have proper and ongoing training; that the pharmacy uses active pharmaceutical

---

[39]NABP will also assist the New Jersey Division of Consumer Affairs with inspections of New Jersey pharmacies engaged in the practice of compounding under a recently reached agreement with the New Jersey Division of Consumer Affairs and the state's Attorney General. New Jersey licenses approximately 40 retail pharmacies that perform sterile compounding and 109 hospital pharmacies that may compound sterile products. NABP inspectors will assist the division in performing field inspections at compounding pharmacies, detailed audits of their records, and in-depth analysis of inspection findings. In addition, NABP inspectors will assist with investigations into complaints about compounding pharmacies, and in bringing charges against any found to be noncompliant.

[40]NABP's Model State Pharmacy Act and Model Rules (Model Act) provide state boards of pharmacy with model language that may be used when developing state laws or board rules. The Model Act includes sections on the boards of pharmacy, licensing (pharmacists, technicians, and facilities), and discipline. NABP last updated the Model State Pharmacy Act and Model Rules in August 2012.

[41]The following national pharmacy organizations established PCAB and, with the exception of the National Association of Boards of Pharmacy, currently make up PCAB's Board of Directors: American College of Apothecaries, National Community Pharmacists Association, American Pharmacists Association, National Alliance of State Pharmacy Associations, International Academy of Compounding Pharmacists, National Home Infusion Association, National Association of Boards of Pharmacy, and the United States Pharmacopeial Convention.

ingredients and inactive materials from appropriate suppliers; that all compounding procedures are fully documented and carried out in conformance with established formulas; and USP standards for compounding. According to a PCAB official, as of June 26, 2013, 176 drug compounding pharmacies received PCAB accreditation, and 124 additional drug compounding pharmacies have applied for PCAB accreditation.[42]

Resource Constraints and Other Factors May Affect States' Ability to Oversee Drug Compounding

Some states may lack the fiscal or staff resources to provide the necessary oversight of drug compounding. A number of officials from state boards of pharmacy attending a December 2012 meeting conducted by FDA expressed confidence that their states had adequate resources to oversee drug compounders, but were concerned about resources in other states. They explained that, until recently, they depended on the states where the pharmacies were located to license and regulate those pharmacies. However, many state budgets have been cut and it is uncertain whether all states have the resources or qualified staff to inspect and otherwise appropriately oversee their licensed pharmacies. The effect of limited state resources may reach across state lines, and it may not be correct to assume that a pharmacy licensed by another state is being regulated adequately.

In addition, differences in pharmacy inspection practices among states may affect oversight of drug compounding in other states. For example, each of the four states we reviewed require licensure or registration of nonresident pharmacies that provide pharmacy services to users in the state, and they require nonresident pharmacies applying for a license or registration to have a current license, permit, or registration issued by the regulatory authority of their home state. The states in our review also have generally relied on the home states of the nonresident pharmacies to inspect these pharmacies on a regular basis. However, state officials and officials from national pharmacy organizations we interviewed told us that the frequency of pharmacy inspections and the qualifications of the pharmacy inspectors vary widely among states, and it is uncertain whether all nonresident pharmacies receive adequate oversight from their home states. Of the four states in our review, one required annual

---

[42]According to a PCAB official, as of June 24, 2013, 176 PCAB-accredited pharmacies were located in 41 states and no state or other entity required PCAB accreditation for a pharmacy to compound drugs.

inspections of all pharmacies located in the state and one required annual inspections of all sterile drug compounding pharmacies located in the state, while another required routine inspections of retail pharmacies in the state once every 4 years. In addition, three of the four states required all pharmacy inspectors to have a license to practice pharmacy in that state, while one state reported having some inspectors without pharmacist licenses.

Officials representing several national pharmacy organizations that we interviewed also expressed concerns regarding whether states have enough resources to regulate and inspect pharmacies on a timely basis. Instead, some states inspect pharmacies only in response to a problem they become aware of through a complaint or adverse drug event. Some of these officials also expressed concern regarding FDA's resources to oversee drug compounding. For example, officials from NABP told us that both FDA and the state boards of pharmacy need more resources for the oversight of drug compounding. Recognizing the need for additional resources to oversee drug compounders, the bill that the California legislature is considering—a bill that would require nonresident pharmacies shipping sterile compounded drugs into the state to have an on-site inspection by the California Board of Pharmacy prior to licensure—would also require those pharmacies to pay for inspection-related travel expenses.

Conclusions

To ensure that compounding pharmacies receive adequate oversight, it is essential to have clear roles for FDA and states regarding the regulation and oversight of drug compounding. The inconsistent federal circuit court decisions complicate FDA's ability to oversee drug compounding by requiring FDA to approach the regulation of drug compounding differently in different parts of the country. In addition, state approaches to the oversight of pharmacies, including compounding pharmacies, vary depending upon each state's regulations and the resources each state devotes to licensing and inspecting its pharmacies. Taken together, the different regulatory approaches FDA must take and the variation in how states oversee drug compounding, create gaps in oversight, which could lead to inadequate assurance that public health is protected.

To adequately carry out the oversight of compounded drugs, FDA must have data systems in place to produce timely, reliable information on inspections, the findings of those inspections, and enforcement actions taken related to compounded drugs. Without reliable, timely data, the agency will not have the information needed to intercede and protect

Americans from unnecessary harm when problems are identified. Recent FDA inspections of 31 entities that produce compounded drugs and the subsequent drug recalls highlight the potential risk to public health of failing to oversee these types of entities.

At the same time that FDA lacks complete information on inspections and enforcement actions taken related to compounded drugs, entities that compound drugs may register as manufacturers in the agency's registration database, and some advertise themselves as FDA-registered. As a result, states and purchasers may incorrectly assume that FDA has approved the products and inspected the facilities for compliance with good manufacturing practices.

Matter for Congressional Consideration

To help ensure appropriate oversight of the safety of products from the entities that prepare and distribute compounded drugs that have a high potential to adversely affect public health, Congress should consider clarifying FDA's authority to regulate entities that compound drugs.

Recommendations for Executive Action

We recommend that the Secretary of Health and Human Services direct the Commissioner of the FDA to

- take steps to consistently collect reliable and timely information in FDA's existing databases on inspections and enforcement actions associated with compounded drugs, and

- clearly differentiate in FDA's database, those manufacturers of FDA-approved drugs that FDA inspects for compliance with good manufacturing practices from those entities compounding drugs that are not FDA-approved and that FDA does not routinely inspect.

Agency Comments and Our Evaluation

We provided a draft of this report to HHS, which oversees FDA, for comment. HHS provided written comments, which are reprinted in appendix III, and technical comments, which we incorporated as appropriate. HHS stated that our report accurately details the limitations associated with FDA's current authority to oversee drug compounding. HHS's comments also support the Matter for Congressional Consideration that Congress should consider clarifying FDA's authority to oversee entities that compound drugs.

HHS neither agreed nor disagreed with our recommendations. Regarding our first recommendation to direct FDA to consistently collect reliable and timely information in FDA's existing databases on inspections and enforcement actions associated with compounded drugs, HHS stated that although FDA's FACTS database can be improved to better aggregate data and to facilitate evaluation of compounding pharmacy activities, these deficiencies do not materially impact FDA's ability to protect the public from harm when problems are identified. We understand that FDA has the ability to access the data associated with compounded drugs by searching under a company name or requesting information across FDA centers and offices; however, as our report notes, FDA lacks ready access to all of the data and lacks the ability to run queries or aggregate the data. For example, when we requested the final inspection classifications for 194 inspections of compounding pharmacies, FDA could not provide this information because, according to FDA officials, the FACTS database does not contain all of the final decisions and obtaining all of the final inspection classifications would require time-consuming manual searches of information maintained in hard copy. As a result, we could not ascertain how many of these inspections found problems that were significant enough for FDA to determine that official action was indicated. Therefore, we continue to believe that FDA should take steps to consistently collect reliable and timely information in its databases on inspections and enforcement actions associated with compounded drugs. Doing so would provide the agency with ready access to key data to inform its decision making on its oversight priorities and allow it to take appropriate action when problems are identified. In its comments, HHS stated that FDA will take steps to further improve its databases to ensure that inspections and actions regarding compounding going forward are coded consistently and are more readily identifiable through electronic searches, and that the final classification for inspections of drug compounders are entered into the FACTS database. These steps are consistent with our recommendation.

Regarding our second recommendation, HHS stated that FDA will consider whether it would be possible or appropriate to differentiate in its database those compounding pharmacies that register voluntarily from conventional manufacturers of FDA-approved drugs that are required to register. These conventional manufacturers are already subject to routine inspections by FDA and are required to list the FDA-approved products they manufacture. Therefore, these entities should already be known to FDA. HHS also commented that FDA will provide information to the public about what it means—and does not mean—to voluntarily register with FDA. HHS further stated that FDA has recommended that Congress require pharmacies engaged in nontraditional compounding in the United States to register with FDA and list the drugs they are compounding, all of which is consistent with our recommendation.

As agreed with your offices, unless you publicly announce the contents of this report earlier, we plan no further distribution until 30 days from the report date. At that time, we will send copies of this report to the Secretary of Health and Human Services, appropriate congressional committees, and other interested parties. In addition, the report will be available at no charge on the GAO Web site at http://www.gao.gov.

If you or your staffs have any questions about this report, please contact me at (202) 512-7114 or crossem@gao.gov. Contact points for our Offices of Congressional Relations and Public Affairs are on the last page of this report. GAO staff who made major contributions to this report are listed in appendix IV.

Marcia Crosse
Director, Health Care

Appendix I: Information on Selection Criteria for Four States

To identify actions planned or taken by states, we interviewed representatives of the state pharmacy regulatory bodies from four states: California, Connecticut, Florida, and Iowa. We chose these states to provide insight into how a range of states approach the oversight of drug compounding; however, the approaches and experiences of these states are not generalizable to all 50 states.

We selected these states to reflect a range of characteristics, including census region, population, number of licensed pharmacies, and variation in compounding regulations. Table 1 lists select data for each selected state.

Table 1: Characteristics Considered in Selecting Four States for Inclusion in Review of State Oversight of Compounding Pharmacies

State	Census region[a]	2010 population (in millions)[b]	Number of compliance officers/ inspectors	Number of state licensed pharmacies	Number of pharmacy license categories[c]	Anticipatory compounding requirements[d]
California	West, Pacific	37.3	37[e]	7,352 (of which 482 are nonresident)[e]	6	May compound in advance of receipt of a patient-specific prescription based on a documented history of prescriptions for the individual patients in that patient population, but only in amounts necessary to ensure continuity of care for that patient population.
Connecticut	Northeast, New England	3.6	10 (8 inspectors and 2 supervisors)[e]	1,301 (of which 624 are nonresident)[e]	6	May compound in anticipation of prescriptions based on routine, regularly-observed prescribing patterns.
Florida	South, South Atlantic	18.8	20[f]	8,050 (of which 754 are nonresident)[f]	16	May compound in anticipation of prescriptions based on routine regularly-observed prescribing patterns.
Iowa	Midwest, West, North Central	3.0	7[f]	1,510 (of which 567 are nonresident)[f,g]	4	May compound drugs prior to receiving a valid prescription based on a history of receiving valid prescriptions generated solely within an established pharmacist/patient/ prescriber relationship.

Source: GAO analysis of U.S. Census Bureau, the National Association of Boards of Pharmacy, and state pharmacy law data.

[a]U.S. Census Bureau, Census Regions.

[b]U.S. Census Bureau, 2010 state demographic profiles.

[c]The National Association of Boards of Pharmacy 2013 Survey of Pharmacy Law.

[d]Analysis of state pharmacy laws and regulations.

[e]As of April 2013.

[f]As of May 2013.

[g]The number of licensed nonresident pharmacies varies over time as new pharmacies are licensed by the state and as licensed pharmacies go out of business or otherwise discontinue their licenses.

Appendix II: History of the Food and Drug Administration's (FDA) Authority over Drug Compounding and Approach to Oversight

Amendments to the Federal Food, Drug, and Cosmetic Act (FDCA) enacted in 1997, and a series of federal court decisions regarding the validity of those amendments, have resulted in several significant shifts in FDA's authority and approach to the regulation of drug compounding over the last two decades. Differences in these court decisions have resulted in inconsistent FDA authority to oversee drug compounding, which, according to the agency, has prompted it to apply three different regulatory approaches to compounded drugs depending upon the federal court jurisdiction in which the drugs are compounded. This appendix describes these legal developments.

1992-1997: Administrative Framework Established for Drug Compounding Oversight

In 1992, FDA issued a compliance policy guide that articulated the agency's approach to applying the FDCA's new drug, adulteration, and misbranding provisions to compounded drugs.[1] FDA noted its longstanding policy of deferring to state regulation of pharmacies engaged in traditional compounding activities, but that it was issuing the compliance policy guide to identify those circumstances under which the agency believed establishments with retail pharmacy licenses were engaged in "manufacturing, distributing, and promoting unapproved new drugs" in a manner outside the traditional pharmacy practice of compounding.[2] According to the 1992 compliance policy guide, the agency might exercise its enforcement discretion to take action against such establishments for violations of the FDCA's new drug approval, adulteration, and misbranding provisions.

---

[1]FDA, Compliance Policy Guides, § 460.200 Manufacture, Distribution, and Promotion of Adulterated, Misbranded, or Unapproved New Drugs for Human Use by State-Licensed Pharmacies (Mar. 16, 1992).

[2]The compliance policy guide describes such traditional compounding to include compounding of "reasonable quantities of drugs upon receipt of a valid prescription for an individually identified patient from a licensed practitioner."

Appendix II: History of the Food and Drug
Administration's (FDA) Authority over Drug
Compounding and Approach to Oversight

1997-2001: Statutory Framework Established for Drug Compounding Oversight

In 1997, Congress passed and the President signed into law the Food and Drug Administration Modernization Act of 1997 (FDAMA) that, among other things, amended the FDCA to expressly permit drug compounding under certain conditions and to exempt compounded drugs meeting these conditions from certain provisions of the FDCA. In particular, under section 503A of the FDCA, as enacted by FDAMA, compounded drugs meeting these conditions were expressly exempt from the requirement that a drug be manufactured in conformity with current good manufacturing practice; that a drug's labeling carry adequate directions for use; and that the drug is the subject of an approved new drug application. To qualify for these exemptions, the pharmacist, physician, or pharmacy compounding the drug had to meet certain criteria, including refraining from advertising, promoting, or soliciting prescriptions for the compounding of any drug.

1999-2002: Judicial Developments in the Ninth Circuit

Shortly after FDAMA's enactment, a group of seven pharmacies challenged section 503A's advertising, promotion, and solicitation restrictions in federal district court, alleging that these restrictions violated the Free Speech Clause of the First Amendment. Agreeing with the plaintiffs, the U.S. District Court for the District of Nevada invalidated section 503A's advertising, promotion, and solicitation restrictions, severing these restrictions from the remainder of section 503A.[3] In 2001, the U.S. Court of Appeals for the Ninth Circuit affirmed the district court's First Amendment holding; however, the Ninth Circuit took the view that Congress would not have enacted section 503A without the advertising, promotion, and solicitation provisions and, therefore, the law's advertising, promotion, and solicitation provisions were not severable. As a result, it held that section 503A, in its entirety, was invalid.[4] In April 2002, the United States Supreme Court in *Thompson v. Western States Medical Center* affirmed the Ninth Circuit's ruling invalidating section 503A's advertising, promotion, and solicitation provisions.[5] Because neither the government nor the pharmacies appealed the Ninth Circuit's

---

[3]*W. States Med. Ctr. v. Shalala*, 69 F. Supp. 2d 1288 (D. Nev. Sept. 16, 1999).

[4]*W. States Med. Ctr. v. Shalala*, 238 F.3d 1090 (9th Cir. Feb. 6, 2001).

[5]*Thompson v. W. States Med. Ctr.*, 535 U.S. 357 (2002).

Appendix II: History of the Food and Drug
Administration's (FDA) Authority over Drug
Compounding and Approach to Oversight

severability ruling, the Supreme Court declined to address the validity of the remaining nonadvertising portions of section 503A.[6]

2002: Revised Administrative Framework for Drug Compounding Oversight

One month after the Supreme Court's ruling in *Western States*, FDA revised its longstanding 1992 *Compliance Policy Guide* on pharmacy compounding to provide "immediate guidance on what types of compounding might be subject to enforcement action under current law."[7] In that guidance, FDA took the position based on the Ninth Circuit's and Supreme Court's *Western States Medical Center* decisions, that "all of section 503A is now invalid." Accordingly, the agency determined it was necessary to issue guidance outlining the factors the agency would consider in taking enforcement action against a compounding pharmacy for violations of the FDCA. In particular, the agency stated that it would continue to defer to state pharmacy authorities for "less significant" violations of the FDCA but that when a pharmacy's activities resemble those of a drug manufacturer it would consider enforcement action. The compliance policy guide provides a nonexhaustive list of such activities. The compliance policy guide reflected FDA's view that, even if a compounding pharmacy has not engaged in these activities, the drugs it compounded would be subject to all of the FDCA's requirements that apply to manufactured drugs; in the compliance policy guide FDA simply outlined those circumstances under which the agency would actually enforce these requirements against a compounding pharmacy.

2006-2008: Judicial Developments in the Fifth Circuit

Four years later, in 2006, a group of 10 pharmacies challenged FDA's authority to regulate compounded drugs. In that case, FDA asserted that compounded drugs fall within the FDCA's definition of "new drug" and, therefore, are subject to those provisions of the act that apply to such drugs.[8] The U.S. District Court for the Western District of Texas disagreed with the agency, holding that compounded drugs when created for an

---

[6]*Id.* at 360.

[7]FDA, Compliance Policy Guide § 460.200 Pharmacy Compounding (May 29, 2002).

[8]Section 201(p) of the FDCA defines "new drug" as "Any drug ... the composition of which is such that such drug is not generally recognized, among experts qualified by scientific training and experience to evaluate the safety and effectiveness of drugs, as safe and effective for use under the conditions prescribed, recommended, or suggested in the labeling thereof." 21 U.S.C. § 321(p).

Appendix II: History of the Food and Drug
Administration's (FDA) Authority over Drug
Compounding and Approach to Oversight

individual patient pursuant to a prescription from a licensed practitioner "are implicitly exempt" from the FDCA's new drug definition and the new drug approval process.[9] On appeal, the U.S. Court of Appeals for the Fifth Circuit reversed the district court's determination and held that compounded drugs are "new drugs" under the FDCA.[10] The court reasoned that Congress would not have enacted FDAMA's provisions exempting compounded drugs from certain of the FDCA's "new drug" requirements had these provisions not applied to compounded drugs in the first instance.[11] To reach this conclusion, the Fifth Circuit considered the severability of section 503A's nonadvertising provisions.[12] Disagreeing with the Ninth Circuit's *Western States* reasoning that Congress would not have enacted section 503A without the advertising provisions, the Fifth Circuit found that the FDCA contained a severability provision and that this provision applied to section 503A. Finding no strong evidence that Congress would not have enacted section 503A without the advertising provisions, the court ruled that the law's nonadvertising provisions were severable from its unconstitutional provisions.[13] The result of the Fifth Circuit's decision is that—at least in the Fifth Circuit—compounded drugs are, in fact, "new drugs" under the FDCA; however, these drugs are expressly exempt from certain requirements that apply to "new drugs"—namely, compliance with current good manufacturing practice, certain labeling requirements, and new drug approval requirements—if they comply with the nonadvertising conditions set forth in section 503A.[14]

---

[9]*Med. Ctr. Pharmacy v. Gonzales*, 451 F. Supp. 2d 854, 863, 865 (D.W.D. Tex. Aug. 30, 2006).

[10]The Fifth Circuit vacated the district court's judgment and remanded the case to the district court for further proceedings. *Med. Ctr. Pharmacy v. Mukasey*, 536 F.3d 383, 409 (5th Cir. Jul. 18, 2008).

[11]*Id.* at 400 ("In 1997, Congress enacted FDAMA as an amendment to the FDCA. That amendment provides considerable evidence that Congress sought to address pharmacy compounding directly and that it did so with the assumption that the 'new drug' provision applies to drugs created through pharmacy compounding.")

[12]*Id.* at 401 ("[T]o rely on FDAMA in construing the 'new drug' definition, we first must address FDAMA's validity.").

[13]*Id.* at 402, 404-05.

[14]*Id.* at 405.

Appendix II: History of the Food and Drug
Administration's (FDA) Authority over Drug
Compounding and Approach to Oversight

2008-Present: FDA's Different Oversight Approaches Following a Circuit Split

The Ninth Circuit Court of Appeals' 2001 *Western States* decision invalidating all of section 503A and the Fifth Circuit Court of Appeals' 2008 *Medical Center Pharmacy* decision holding that all of section 503A other than the advertising, promotion, and solicitation restrictions is valid are directly at odds. As a result of these decisions, section 503A is invalid in those states in the Ninth Circuit (Alaska, Arizona, California, Hawaii, Idaho, Montana, Nevada, Oregon, and Washington) and in full force and effect in those states in the Fifth Circuit (Louisiana, Mississippi, and Texas). FDA officials described the agency's approach to regulating compounded drugs under this incongruous legal landscape as follows:

- In the Ninth Circuit, the agency takes the approach that all compounded drugs are "new drugs" under the FDCA, and the agency determines whether to consider taking enforcement action against a compounding pharmacy based on whether the pharmacy engages in any of the activities outlined in the agency's 2002 compliance policy guide on drug compounding. Even if a compounding pharmacy has not engaged in the activities outlined in the compliance policy guide, the drugs it compounds are, as a legal matter, subject to all of the FDCA requirements that apply to "new drugs"; the compliance policy guide simply outlines those circumstances under which the agency will consider enforcing these requirements against a compounding pharmacy.[15]

- In the Fifth Circuit, FDA determines whether a compounded drug meets section 503A's exemption from certain FDCA requirements that would preclude the agency from taking enforcement action against a drug compounder for noncompliance with these requirements.

- For compounding pharmacies outside of the Fifth and Ninth Circuits, which is the majority of the country, the agency applies the criteria in both section 503A and its 2002 compliance policy guide to determine whether to take enforcement action.

Table 2 identifies the criteria that a compounded drug must meet to qualify for the exemption under section 503A of the FDCA from certain of the law's requirements and the criteria in FDA's 2002 compliance policy

---

[15]The Ninth Circuit Court of Appeals decision also applies to FDA's authority over certain compounding pharmacies located in Colorado, New Jersey, Tennessee, Texas, and Wisconsin, as these pharmacies were party to the *Western States* lawsuit.

guide, which the agency considers in determining whether to take enforcement action against an entity engaged in drug compounding.

Table 2: Comparison of the Food and Drug Administration's (FDA) Authority and Oversight of Drug Compounding under Section 503A of the Federal Food, Drug, and Cosmetic Act (FDCA) and FDA's 2002 Compliance Policy Guide

Section 503A: A drug compounded according to each of the criteria is exempt from three key requirements under the FDCA.[a]	2002 Compliance Policy Guide: In determining whether to initiate enforcement action against a compounding pharmacy, FDA considers whether the compounding pharmacy has engaged in any of these activities.[b,c,d]
Compounds for an identified individual patient based on the receipt of a valid prescription order or a notation, approved by the prescribing practitioner, on the prescription order that a compounded drug is necessary for the patient. If compounding occurs in anticipation of a prescription, it is based on a history of valid prescription orders for the compounding of the drug product, which orders have been generated solely within an established relationship between the pharmacy and the prescriber or patient.	Compounding in anticipation of receiving prescriptions, except in very limited quantities in relation to the amounts of drugs compounded after receiving valid prescriptions.
Does not compound a drug product that appears on a list published by the Secretary of drug products withdrawn or removed from the market because such drug product or their components have been found to be unsafe or not effective	Compounding drugs withdrawn or removed from the market for safety reasons
Compounds using ingredients (other than bulk drug substances) that comply with an applicable monograph	Receiving, storing, or using drug components not meeting official compendia requirements
Compounds using bulk drug substances that comply with an applicable compendia monograph if one exists; if one does not exist, uses bulk drug substances that are components of FDA-approved drugs or that appear on a list developed by the agency[e]	Compounding finished drugs from certain bulk active ingredients that are not components of FDA approved drugs without an investigational new drug application
Compounds with bulk drug substances that were made in an FDA-registered facility, each of which is accompanied by valid certificates of analysis	Receiving, storing, or using drugs substances without obtaining assurance they were made in an FDA-registered facility
Compounds in a state that has entered into a memorandum of understanding with the Secretary that addresses the distribution of inordinate amounts of compounded drug products interstate and provides for appropriate investigation by a state agency of complaints relating to compounded drug products distributed outside of the state; in the alternative, less than 5 percent of the compounding individual's or entity's total prescription orders are for compounded products distributed out of the state	Compounding drugs for third parties who resell to individual patients or at wholesale to other persons or entities or using commercial scale manufacturing or testing equipment for compounding drug products
Does not compound regularly or in inordinate amounts (as defined by the Secretary) any drug products that are essentially copies of a commercially-available drug product[f]	Compounding drugs that are commercially available or that are essentially copies of commercially-available FDA-approved drug products, except in certain limited circumstances.
Does not compound any drug that is identified by the Secretary by regulation as a drug that presents demonstrable difficulties for compounding that reasonably demonstrate an adverse effect on the safety or effectiveness of that drug	*No comparable criterion*

Section 503A: **A drug compounded according to each of the criteria is exempt from three key requirements under the FDCA.**[a]	**2002 Compliance Policy Guide:** **In determining whether to initiate enforcement action against a compounding pharmacy, FDA considers whether the compounding pharmacy has engaged in any of these activities.**[b,c,d]
The compounding is performed by a licensed pharmacist in a state licensed pharmacy or by a licensed physician.	Failing to operate in conformance with applicable state pharmacy laws

Source: GAO analysis.

Notes: Data are from section 503A of the Federal Food, Drug, and Cosmetic Act and FDA's 2002 compliance policy guide on drug compounding.

Section 503A's advertising, promotion, and solicitation restrictions are not presented here, as the United States Supreme Court declared these provisions unconstitutional. *Thompson v. W. States Med. Ctr.*, 535 U.S. 357 (2002).

[a]FDA applies these criteria to drugs compounded in states other than those in the Ninth Circuit, where section 503A is invalid, to determine whether these drugs are exempt from certain FDCA requirements.

[b]FDA applies these criteria in states outside of the Fifth Circuit to determine whether to initiate enforcement action against a compounding pharmacy in such a state.

[c]For compounding pharmacies outside of the Fifth and Ninth Circuits, FDA applies the criteria in both section 503A and the 2002 compliance policy guide to determine whether to take enforcement action.

[d]In addition to the specific factors outlined in the 2002 compliance policy guide, according to FDA, the agency also considers whether a licensed practitioner has extemporaneously compounded a drug upon receipt of a valid prescription for an individually identified patient in considering whether to take enforcement action.

[e]FDA issued a proposed rule on January 7, 1999, containing a list of bu k drug substances that the agency proposed to permit for use in drug compounding. 64 Fed. Reg. 996 (Jan. 7, 1999). According to FDA, the agency never issued a final rule because of the Ninth Circuit's and Supreme Court's *Western States* decisions. Since the Fifth Circuit Court of Appeals' 2008 *Medical Center Pharmacy* decision, the agency has considered whether to maintain such a list.

[f]The term "essentially a copy of a commercially-available drug product" does not include a drug product in which there is a change, made for an identified individual patient, which produces for that patient a significant difference, as determined by the prescribing practitioner, between the compounded drug and the comparable commercially available drug product.

Appendix III: Comments from the Department of Health and Human Services

DEPARTMENT OF HEALTH & HUMAN SERVICES

OFFICE OF THE SECRETARY

Assistant Secretary for Legislation
Washington, DC 20201

JUL 1 2 2013

Marcia Crosse
Director, Health Care
U.S. Government Accountability Office
441 G Street NW
Washington, DC 20548

Dear Ms. Crosse:

Attached are comments on the U.S. Government Accountability Office's (GAO) report entitled, "DRUG COMPOUNDING: Clear Authority and More Reliable Data Needed to Strengthen FDA Oversight" (GAO 13-702).

The Department appreciates the opportunity to review this report prior to publication.

Sincerely,

Jim R. Esquea
Assistant Secretary for Legislation

Attachment

GENERAL COMMENTS OF THE DEPARTMENT OF HEALTH AND HUMAN SERVICES (HHS) ON THE GOVERNMENT ACCOUNTABILITY OFFICE'S (GAO) DRAFT REPORT ENTITLED, "DRUG COMPOUNDING: CLEAR AUTHORITY AND MORE RELIABLE DATA NEEDED TO STENGTHEN FDA OVERSIGHT" (GAO 13-702)

The Department appreciates the opportunity to review and comment on this draft report. The report accurately details the limitations associated with FDA's current authority. FDA's current authority does not provide the agency with the tools suited to effectively regulate certain drug compounding operations, and the findings in the report support the need for legislation to allow FDA to appropriately regulate this evolving industry.

As GAO notes, in 1997, section 503A of the Federal Food, Drug, and Cosmetic Act attempted to clarify the status of pharmacy compounding under federal law, but subsequent conflicting court decisions resulted in FDA applying different authorities in different parts of the country, and created uncertainty regarding how courts would rule on section 503A in other parts of the country. These court rulings, combined with the perceived limitations and ambiguities in the law, have made difficult and vulnerable to legal challenge FDA's attempts to apply its regulatory and inspectional authority over pharmacies that compound drugs. Similarly, the current patchwork of state laws that differ in prescription requirements and quality control rules also hamper the states' oversight of compounding pharmacies. As GAO notes, differences in inspection practices among states, such as inconsistent requirements regarding the frequency of pharmacy inspections and the qualifications of pharmacy inspectors, and in some cases the lack of fiscal and staff resources, indicate that states lack uniform, consistent, and national standards and adequate resources to provide the necessary oversight of drug compounding.

Since the 1990s, a new breed of specialty pharmacy compounding has evolved that has outgrown the law, and can pose a threat to the health of the public. These pharmacies produce medications in advance of or without obtaining a prescription and distribute them across the country. They make drug products that are intended to be sterile and must be made to exacting standards to prevent dangerous contamination. The magnitude and complexity of these operations have outpaced FDA's authorities, which are not the right fit for FDA to provide appropriate and efficient oversight of this growing industry.

The fungal meningitis outbreak of 2012 serves as a cautionary tale of the public health dangers posed by practices in compounding pharmacies. Tragically, this is only the latest major public health incident relating to pharmacy compounding. These incidents are emblematic of long-standing issues associated with the practice of compounding and highlight the need for appropriate authorities for FDA to effectively protect the public health.

Since the fungal meningitis outbreak, incidents related to unsafe pharmacy compounding practices, including observed contaminated products and patient injuries, recalls of sterile compounded products, and documentation of sterile processing concerns in numerous compounding pharmacies, demonstrate that action must be taken. As GAO notes, in response to this public health threat, FDA used its existing resources and authorities to conduct proactive inspections of 31 firms that are known to have produced sterile compounded drugs in the past. FDA identified these firms using a risk-based model that included factors such as serious adverse event reports, historical inspection data, and reports of product quality problems. The inspections specifically focused on each firm's processing of sterile drugs to identify firms that may pose a

1

<u>**GENERAL COMMENTS OF THE DEPARTMENT OF HEALTH AND HUMAN
SERVICES (HHS) ON THE GOVERNMENT ACCOUNTABILITY OFFICE'S (GAO)
DRAFT REPORT ENTITLED, "DRUG COMPOUNDING: CLEAR AUTHORITY AND
MORE RELIABLE DATA NEEDED TO STENGTHEN FDA OVERSIGHT" (GAO 13-
702)**</u>

higher risk of producing contaminated sterile products. During these proactive inspections, as
well as over 30 for-cause inspections conducted recently, FDA documented significant lapses in
sterility practices, inappropriate conditions for sterile processing, and other practices that create
risk of contamination. FDA has conducted 62 inspections so far in fiscal year 2013 and issued
inspection observation reports (FDA Form 483s) on 52 of those that list objectionable conditions
observed at the facilities. As noted on some of these 483s, select FDA observations during the
inspections include: unidentified black particles floating in vials of supposedly sterile medicine;
rust and mold in "clean rooms" where sterile injectable medications were produced; technicians
handling supposedly sterile products with bare hands; and employees wearing non-sterile lab
coats. In part, due to FDA's observations noted during the inspections, several firms have
voluntarily recalled their products, and others temporarily suspended production of their products
intended to be sterile while they correct deficiencies found by the investigators.

Even in light of the recent tragic events, some of these firms challenged FDA's authority to
conduct these inspections. In at least six instances, firms delayed the inspections or denied FDA
inspectors full access to records or observation of their sterile processing activities at some of
these facilities. After some initial delay, and in some instances, discussion with the firms' legal
counsels, these firms eventually provided the investigators the necessary access to inspect their
facilities. In two other instances, FDA had to get administrative warrants from the courts,
resulting in U.S. Marshals accompanying FDA inspectors back to the firms so FDA could
complete the inspections.

The agency is currently evaluating the information obtained during the inspections and where
applicable, will apply its existing legal authority to protect the public health, but it is unclear
whether FDA will be successful in obtaining appropriate corrective actions in all cases.
The Administration is committed to working with Congress to address the threat to public health
from limitations in authorities for effective oversight of certain compounding practices. To that
end, FDA has developed a framework that could serve as the basis for the development of a risk-
based program to protect the public health.

Risk-Based Framework

Recognizing the history of compounding practice, FDA supports the long-standing policy that all
compounding should be performed in a licensed pharmacy by a licensed pharmacist (or a
licensed physician), and that there must be a medical need for the compounded drug.
Further, we believe there should be a distinction between two categories of compounding:
traditional and non-traditional. Traditional compounding would include the combining, mixing,
or altering of ingredients to create a customized medication for an individual patient with an
individualized medical need for the compounded product, in response to a valid patient-specific
prescription or order from a licensed practitioner documenting such medical need. Traditional
compounding, while posing some risk, plays an important role in the health care system, and
should remain the subject of state regulation of the practice of pharmacy.

2

<u>**GENERAL COMMENTS OF THE DEPARTMENT OF HEALTH AND HUMAN
SERVICES (HHS) ON THE GOVERNMENT ACCOUNTABILITY OFFICE'S (GAO)
DRAFT REPORT ENTITLED, "DRUG COMPOUNDING: CLEAR AUTHORITY AND
MORE RELIABLE DATA NEEDED TO STENGTHEN FDA OVERSIGHT" (GAO 13-
702)**</u>

Non-traditional compounding would include certain types of compounding for which there is a
medical need, but that pose higher risks. FDA proposes working with Congress to define non-
traditional compounding based on factors that make the product higher risk, such as any sterile
compounding in advance of or without receiving a prescription, where the drug is distributed out
of the state in which it was produced. Non-traditional compounding would be subject to federal
standards adequate to ensure that the compounding could be performed without putting patients
at undue risk, and FDA would inspect against and enforce these federal standards. Such a
definition focuses on the highest risk activities and offers a uniform degree of protection across
all 50 states, for highest-risk compounding activities.

Non-traditional compounding should, because of the higher risk presented, be subject to a greater
degree of oversight. Sterile products produced in advance of or without a prescription and
shipped interstate should be subject to the highest level of controls, established by FDA and
appropriate to the activity, similar to current Good Manufacturing Practice (cGMP) standards
applicable to conventional drug manufacturers.

In addition, FDA believes that with noted exceptions, certain products are not appropriate for
compounding under any circumstances. These products would include: 1) what are essentially
copies of FDA-approved drugs, absent the drug appearing on FDA's shortage list; and 2)
complex dosage forms such as extended release products; transdermal patches; liposomal
products; most biologics; and other products as designated by FDA. Producing complex dosage
forms would require an approved application and compliance with cGMP standards, along with
other requirements applicable to manufactured drug products.

FDA believes that there are other authorities that would be important to support this new
regulatory paradigm. For example, FDA should have clear ability to collect and test samples of
compounded drugs and to examine and collect records in a compounding pharmacy, just as the
agency does when inspecting other manufacturers. FDA should also have clear ability to
examine records such as records of prescriptions received, products shipped, volume of
operations, and operational records such as batch records, product quality test results, and
stability testing results. Such inspections are necessary to determine when a pharmacy exceeds
the bounds of traditional compounding, to respond to public health threats, and to enforce federal
standards.

FDA also believes that an accurate inventory of pharmacies engaged in non-traditional
compounding would facilitate appropriate oversight and coordination with state regulators. In
addition, FDA looks forward to working with the Congress on potential improvements that may
include label statements and adverse event reporting that have proven useful in other areas. A
user-fee-funded regulatory program may be appropriate to support the inspections and other
oversight activities outlined in this framework. We look forward to working with Congress to
explore the appropriate funding mechanisms to support this work, which could include
registration or other fees, as Congress has authorized and FDA has successfully implemented in
other settings.

3

<u>GENERAL COMMENTS OF THE DEPARTMENT OF HEALTH AND HUMAN
SERVICES (HHS) ON THE GOVERNMENT ACCOUNTABILITY OFFICE'S (GAO)
DRAFT REPORT ENTITLED, "DRUG COMPOUNDING: CLEAR AUTHORITY AND
MORE RELIABLE DATA NEEDED TO STENGTHEN FDA OVERSIGHT" (GAO 13-
702)</u>

Response to GAO Conclusions and Recommendations

In this report, GAO raises concerns about FDA's inspection database, the Field
Accomplishments and Compliance Tracking System (FACTS), and states that "FDA lacks
reliable data to make decisions to prioritize its inspection workload and other follow-up and
enforcement actions" with respect to compounding pharmacies. Specifically, GAO states that the
coding of some inspections of compounding pharmacies as manufacturers or veterinary drug
compounders and the absence of ready access in the FACTS database to all of the final
inspection classification decisions, would have a significant impact on the agency's ability to
"make decisions on its oversight priorities and to take appropriate action when problems are
identified." GAO concludes that, because FDA does not have timely and reliable access to the
data available in FACTS, the agency is unable to "intercede and protect Americans from
unnecessary harm when problems are identified."

Although FDA recognizes that the FACTS database can be improved to better aggregate data
and facilitate evaluation of compounding pharmacy activities across the limited universe of
compounding pharmacies in the database, FDA maintains that the database deficiencies cited by
GAO in this report do not materially impact the agency's ability to protect the public from harm
when problems are identified. As GAO notes in its report, compounding pharmacies that meet
certain criteria are generally not required to register with FDA or list their products, and,
therefore, FDA does not know who they are and what they are compounding. FDA has
recommended that Congress require pharmacies engaged in non-traditional compounding in the
United States to register with FDA and list the drugs they are compounding so that FDA has
information about who is doing this compounding and what they are producing. FDA would use
this information to prioritize inspections using a risk based model so that it could appropriately
focus its regulatory activities on the highest risk compounding. This would greatly enhance the
agency's ability to provide appropriate oversight of non-traditional compounding practices and
help to protect the public health.

Even with the database as it is currently configured, however, the agency is able to access the
data it has gathered through its inspectional and investigational activities to inform its
inspectional priorities and decision-making regarding compounding pharmacies. FDA employees
can access the inspectional data in FACTS by searching the database using the firm name rather
than a program assignment code, and the database will provide all of the inspectional data on that
firm, regardless of whether an inspection was coded as involving a manufacturer, veterinary
compounder or as an investigation. Additionally, the collaboration between FDA's Center for
Drug Evaluation and Research (CDER) and its Office of Regulatory Affairs (ORA) for
inspections and/or investigations of a compounding pharmacy, assures that all relevant data
gathered by FDA is made available to the decision-makers. For example, CDER makes the final
classification decision on inspections. If the final decision is not in the FACTS database, the
investigator(s) can request that information from CDER as part of their pre-inspection review of
the firm's compliance history, and CDER is able to provide that information from its files.

4

<u>**GENERAL COMMENTS OF THE DEPARTMENT OF HEALTH AND HUMAN
SERVICES (HHS) ON THE GOVERNMENT ACCOUNTABILITY OFFICE'S (GAO)
DRAFT REPORT ENTITLED, "DRUG COMPOUNDING: CLEAR AUTHORITY AND
MORE RELIABLE DATA NEEDED TO STENGTHEN FDA OVERSIGHT" (GAO 13-
702)**</u>

GAO specifically recommends that FDA take steps to consistently collect reliable information in
its databases on inspections and enforcement actions, and that it differentiate in its databases
those manufacturers of FDA-approved drugs that it inspects for compliance with good
manufacturing practices from those manufacturers compounding drugs that are not FDA-
approved and that FDA does not routinely inspect.

As noted above, FDA is working with Congress on legislation to require non-traditional
compounders to register and list. In addition, FDA will take steps to further improve its
databases to ensure that inspections and actions regarding compounding going forward are coded
consistently and are more readily identifiable through electronic searches, and that the final
classification for inspections of drug compounders are entered into the FACTS database. FDA
also will consider whether it would be possible and appropriate to differentiate in its database
those compounding pharmacies that register voluntarily from conventional manufacturers that
are required to register, and will provide information to the public about what it means and does
not mean to voluntarily register with the FDA.

5

Appendix IV: GAO Contact and Staff Acknowledgments

GAO Contact	Marcia Crosse, (202) 512-7114 or crossem@gao.gov
Staff Acknowledgments	In addition to the contact named above, Kim Yamane, Assistant Director; Matthew Byer; Sandra George; Drew Long; and Lisa A. Lusk made key contributions to this report.

GAO's Mission	The Government Accountability Office, the audit, evaluation, and investigative arm of Congress, exists to support Congress in meeting its constitutional responsibilities and to help improve the performance and accountability of the federal government for the American people. GAO examines the use of public funds; evaluates federal programs and policies; and provides analyses, recommendations, and other assistance to help Congress make informed oversight, policy, and funding decisions. GAO's commitment to good government is reflected in its core values of accountability, integrity, and reliability.
Obtaining Copies of GAO Reports and Testimony	The fastest and easiest way to obtain copies of GAO documents at no cost is through GAO's website (http://www.gao.gov). Each weekday afternoon, GAO posts on its website newly released reports, testimony, and correspondence. To have GAO e-mail you a list of newly posted products, go to http://www.gao.gov and select "E-mail Updates."
Order by Phone	The price of each GAO publication reflects GAO's actual cost of production and distribution and depends on the number of pages in the publication and whether the publication is printed in color or black and white. Pricing and ordering information is posted on GAO's website, http://www.gao.gov/ordering.htm. Place orders by calling (202) 512-6000, toll free (866) 801-7077, or TDD (202) 512-2537. Orders may be paid for using American Express, Discover Card, MasterCard, Visa, check, or money order. Call for additional information.
Connect with GAO	Connect with GAO on Facebook, Flickr, Twitter, and YouTube. Subscribe to our RSS Feeds or E-mail Updates. Listen to our Podcasts. Visit GAO on the web at www.gao.gov.
To Report Fraud, Waste, and Abuse in Federal Programs	Contact: Website: http://www.gao.gov/fraudnet/fraudnet.htm E-mail: fraudnet@gao.gov Automated answering system: (800) 424-5454 or (202) 512-7470
Congressional Relations	Katherine Siggerud, Managing Director, siggerudk@gao.gov, (202) 512-4400, U.S. Government Accountability Office, 441 G Street NW, Room 7125, Washington, DC 20548
Public Affairs	Chuck Young, Managing Director, youngc1@gao.gov, (202) 512-4800 U.S. Government Accountability Office, 441 G Street NW, Room 7149 Washington, DC 20548

Please Print on Recycled Paper.

www.ingramcontent.com/pod-product-compliance
Lightning Source LLC
Chambersburg PA
CBHW080614290526
45790CB00007B/2774